Introduction:

A while back, there were... two people who didn't know each other. Now they can't imagine life without each other. The story of how it happened is special for everyone, but always precious to look back at!

This journal prompts you to write your story down. With .... questions for couples, you can reminisce tenderly about the past, create a capsule of your relationship as it is right now and excitedly contemplate the future.

This journal is a way to , share with your partner, each day for 365 days, with a daily question, it will guide you to link with each other through memories, hopes, thoughts, dreams, viewpoints, preferences, flights of fancy, and your own special essence. If you already know each other well, this journal will strengthen your bond by giving you a daily touchpoint.

So enjoy sharing and comparing your responses as you get to know each other better!

About us:

Our new name is:_____

_____

First meet Date:_____ Location:_____

Who said "I love you" first?_____

What we loved most about our wedding day:

You_____

Me_____

Insert a Picture

01 JANUARY

What's your ideal way to spend a vacation?

20____:_____

_____

_____

_____

_____

_____

20____:_____

_____

_____

_____

_____

_____

20____:_____

_____

_____

_____

_____

JANUARY

02

What makes you dislike a person?

20_____:_____

_____

_____

_____

_____

20_____:_____

_____

_____

_____

_____

20_____:_____

_____

_____

_____

03 JANUARY

Do you think you are a confident person? Why or why not?

20____:_____

_____

_____

_____

_____

20____:_____

_____

_____

_____

_____

20____:_____

_____

_____

_____

_____

 # JANUARY

 **04**

What about yourself are you most proud of?

20____:_____

_____

_____

_____

_____

20____:_____

_____

_____

_____

_____

20____:_____

_____

_____

_____

_____

05 JANUARY

What would the best version of you be like?

20____:_____

_____

_____

_____

_____

20____:_____

_____

_____

_____

_____

20____:_____

_____

_____

_____

_____

What life experiences did you miss out on?

20____: _____

_____

_____

_____

_____

_____

20____: _____

_____

_____

_____

_____

_____

20____: _____

_____

_____

_____

_____

07 JANUARY

When are you the most "you"?

20____:_____
_____
_____
_____
_____
_____

20____:_____
_____
_____
_____
_____
_____

20____:_____
_____
_____
_____
_____

JANUARY

08

What musical instrument do you wish
you could play?

20____:_____

_____

_____

_____

_____

20____:_____

_____

_____

_____

_____

20____:_____

_____

_____

_____

09 JANUARY

What is the nicest compliment you've received?

20____:
_____
_____
_____
_____
_____
_____

20____:
_____
_____
_____
_____
_____
_____

20____:
_____
_____
_____
_____

JANUARY

10

What age would you like to live to?

20____:_____

_____

_____

_____

_____

20____:_____

_____

_____

_____

_____

20____:_____

_____

_____

_____

11 JANUARY

How did you fall out with some of your
previously close friends?

20____:_____

_____

_____

_____

_____

20____:_____

_____

_____

_____

_____

20____:_____

_____

_____

_____

JANUARY 12

When has a mundane occurrence or chance completely changed the course of your life?

20____:_____

_____

_____

_____

_____

20____:_____

_____

_____

_____

_____

20____:_____

_____

_____

_____

_____

13 JANUARY

Are you happy with the people you surround yourself with? Why or why not?

20____:_____

_____

_____

_____

_____

_____

20____:_____

_____

_____

_____

_____

_____

20____:_____

_____

_____

_____

_____

JANUARY 14

If you could travel to any country in
the world for one month, where would
you go?

20___:_____
_____
_____
_____
_____
_____

20___:_____
_____
_____
_____
_____
_____

20___:_____
_____
_____
_____
_____

15 JANUARY

What is your favorite memory of someone who isn't in your life anymore?

20____:_____

_____

_____

_____

_____

_____

20____:_____

_____

_____

_____

_____

_____

20____:_____

_____

_____

_____

_____

_____

JANUARY

How superstitious are you?

20_____:_____
_____
_____
_____
_____

20_____:_____
_____
_____
_____
_____

20_____:_____
_____
_____
_____
_____

17 JANUARY

What has been a recurring theme in your life?

20____: _____
_____
_____
_____
_____
_____

20____: _____
_____
_____
_____
_____
_____

20____: _____
_____
_____
_____
_____

JANUARY

What was your most inappropriate or embarrassing fart?

20___:_____

_____

_____

_____

_____

20___:_____

_____

_____

_____

_____

20___:_____

_____

_____

_____

_____

19 JANUARY

What do you think happens after death?

20____:_____

_____

_____

_____

_____

20____:_____

_____

_____

_____

_____

20____:_____

_____

_____

_____

_____

JANUARY

20

What are your top 5 rules for life?

20____: _____

_____

_____

_____

_____

_____

20____: _____

_____

_____

_____

_____

_____

20____: _____

_____

_____

_____

_____

21 JANUARY

What's your favorite thing in your / our house?

20____:_____
_____
_____
_____
_____
_____

20____:_____
_____
_____
_____
_____
_____

20____:_____
_____
_____
_____
_____

JANUARY 22

What book or movie do you wish you could experience for the first time again?

20_____:_____

_____

_____

_____

_____

_____

20_____:_____

_____

_____

_____

_____

_____

20_____:_____

_____

_____

_____

_____

_____

23 JANUARY

If you had a friend who spoke to you the same way you speak to yourself, would you keep them as a friend?

20____:_____
_____
_____
_____
_____
_____

20____:_____
_____
_____
_____
_____
_____

20____:_____
_____
_____
_____
_____

JANUARY 24

What petty thing that people do really gets on your nerves?

20____: _____

_____

_____

_____

_____

20____: _____

_____

_____

_____

_____

20____: _____

_____

_____

_____

25 JANUARY

What brings meaning to your life?

20____:_____

_____

_____

_____

_____

_____

20____:_____

_____

_____

_____

_____

_____

20____:_____

_____

_____

_____

_____

JANUARY

What is something you wish you could say to people but can't?

20____: _____
_____
_____
_____
_____

20____: _____
_____
_____
_____
_____

20____: _____
_____
_____
_____
_____

27 JANUARY

What are some of the most attractive traits a person can have?

20____: _____

_____

_____

_____

_____

_____

20____: _____

_____

_____

_____

_____

_____

20____: _____

_____

_____

_____

_____

JANUARY

28

What's a secret you've never told anyone?

20___:_____

_____

_____

_____

_____

20___:_____

_____

_____

_____

_____

20___:_____

_____

_____

_____

_____

29 JANUARY

What small pleasures do you enjoy the most?

20_____:_____

_____

_____

_____

_____

_____

20_____:_____

_____

_____

_____

_____

_____

20_____:_____

_____

_____

_____

JANUARY

30

Who is the most irritating person you know?

20____:_____

_____

_____

_____

_____

20____:_____

_____

_____

_____

_____

20____:_____

_____

_____

_____

_____

31 JANUARY

What has been your biggest screw up so far?

20_____:_____

_____

_____

_____

_____

20_____:_____

_____

_____

_____

_____

_____

20_____:_____

_____

_____

_____

_____

FEBRUARY 01

What have you struggled with your entire life?

20___:_____
_____
_____
_____
_____
_____

20___:_____
_____
_____
_____
_____
_____

20___:_____
_____
_____
_____
_____

02 FEBRUARY

What is the most significant change you would like to make in your life?

20_____:_____

_____

_____

_____

_____

20_____:_____

_____

_____

_____

_____

20_____:_____

_____

_____

_____

_____

FEBRUARY 03

What do you want out of life?

20____: _____

_____

_____

_____

_____

20____: _____

_____

_____

_____

_____

20____: _____

_____

_____

_____

04 FEBRUARY

What calms you down the most?

20____: _____
_____
_____
_____
_____
_____

20____: _____
_____
_____
_____
_____
_____

20____: _____
_____
_____
_____
_____

FEBRUARY

What are kinds of things do you find repulsive?

20____:_____

_____

_____

_____

_____

20____:_____

_____

_____

_____

_____

20____:_____

_____

_____

_____

06 FEBRUARY

What would your perfect life look like?

20____:_____

_____

_____

_____

_____

_____

20____:_____

_____

_____

_____

_____

_____

20____:_____

_____

_____

_____

_____

FEBRUARY

If you received a salary to follow whatever passion you wanted to, what would you do?

20____:_____

_____

_____

_____

_____

20____:_____

_____

_____

_____

_____

_____

20____:_____

_____

_____

_____

_____

08 FEBRUARY

What's your most embarrassing story about being sick?

20____:_____
_____
_____
_____
_____
_____

20____:_____
_____
_____
_____
_____
_____

20____:_____
_____
_____
_____
_____

FEBRUARY

What friend have you not thought about in a long time?

20___:_____
_____
_____
_____
_____

20___:_____
_____
_____
_____
_____

20___:_____
_____
_____
_____
_____

10 FEBRUARY

What's the craziest thing that has happened at a job you worked at?

20____:_____

_____

_____

_____

_____

_____

20____:_____

_____

_____

_____

_____

_____

20____:_____

_____

_____

_____

_____

_____

FEBRUARY  11

Who do you act nice around but secretly dislike?

20____:_____

_____

_____

_____

_____

20____:_____

_____

_____

_____

_____

_____

20____:_____

_____

_____

_____

_____

12 FEBRUARY

If money was no object, and with no input from me, how would you decorate your / our house?

20____:_____

_____

_____

_____

_____

20____:_____

_____

_____

_____

_____

20____:_____

_____

_____

_____

_____

FEBRUARY 13

How good are you at reading people?

20____:_____
_____
_____
_____
_____

20____:_____
_____
_____
_____
_____

20____:_____
_____
_____
_____
_____

14 FEBRUARY

Are you hopeful about your future?

20____:_____

_____

_____

_____

_____

20____:_____

_____

_____

_____

_____

20____:_____

_____

_____

_____

_____

FEBRUARY 15

Who do you want to be more like or
who do you look up to most?

20____: _____
_____
_____
_____
_____

20____: _____
_____
_____
_____
_____

20____: _____
_____
_____
_____
_____

16 FEBRUARY

What were the healthiest and unhealthiest periods of your life?

20____: _____

_____

_____

_____

_____

20____: _____

_____

_____

_____

_____

20____: _____

_____

_____

_____

_____

FEBRUARY 17

What's the worst emotional or mental anguish you've endured?

20____:_____

_____

_____

_____

_____

20____:_____

_____

_____

_____

_____

20____:_____

_____

_____

_____

18 FEBRUARY

What do you like most about where we live?

20____:_____

_____

_____

_____

_____

_____

20____:_____

_____

_____

_____

_____

_____

20____:_____

_____

_____

_____

_____

FEBRUARY

19

What do you worry about?

20____:_____

_____

_____

_____

_____

20____:_____

_____

_____

_____

_____

20____:_____

_____

_____

_____

_____

20 FEBRUARY

What's something you screwed up and then tried to hide?

20____:_____

_____

_____

_____

_____

_____

20____:_____

_____

_____

_____

_____

_____

20____:_____

_____

_____

_____

_____

FEBRUARY 21

What's the scariest / creepiest place you have ever been?

20____: _____

_____

_____

_____

_____

20____: _____

_____

_____

_____

_____

20____: _____

_____

_____

_____

_____

22 FEBRUARY

Do you think the world is improving or getting worse? Why?

20_____:_____

_____

_____

_____

_____

_____

20_____:_____

_____

_____

_____

_____

_____

20_____:_____

_____

_____

_____

_____

FEBRUARY 23

How do you think society is changing?
Do you think we'll change with it?

20___:_____

_____

_____

_____

_____

20___:_____

_____

_____

_____

_____

20___:_____

_____

_____

_____

_____

24 FEBRUARY

What's the worst thing that people are proud of?

20____:_____
_____
_____
_____
_____
_____

20____:_____
_____
_____
_____
_____
_____

20____:_____
_____
_____
_____
_____

FEBRUARY 25

What's the biggest betrayal you have ever experienced?

20____: _____

_____

_____

_____

_____

20____: _____

_____

_____

_____

_____

20____: _____

_____

_____

_____

26 FEBRUARY

What would be the greatest gift to receive?

20____:_____

_____

_____

_____

_____

20____:_____

_____

_____

_____

_____

20____:_____

_____

_____

_____

_____

FEBRUARY 27

What is something that you are dreading?

20____:_____

_____

_____

_____

_____

20____:_____

_____

_____

_____

_____

20____:_____

_____

_____

_____

_____

28 FEBRUARY

What makes you feel super fancy?

20_____:_____
_____
_____
_____
_____
_____

20_____:_____
_____
_____
_____
_____
_____

20_____:_____
_____
_____
_____
_____

FEBRUARY

29

What would you want your obituary to say?

20____:_____

_____

_____

_____

_____

20____:_____

_____

_____

_____

_____

20____:_____

_____

_____

_____

_____

01 MARCH

What has taken up too much of your life?

20____:_____
_____
_____
_____
_____

20____:_____
_____
_____
_____
_____

20____:_____
_____
_____
_____

MARCH

What's the most disheartening and heartening realization you have come to?

20____: _____
_____
_____
_____
_____
_____

20____: _____
_____
_____
_____
_____
_____

20____: _____
_____
_____
_____
_____
_____

03 MARCH

What was the hardest lesson you've had to learn?

20____:_____

_____

_____

_____

_____

_____

20____:_____

_____

_____

_____

_____

_____

20____:_____

_____

_____

_____

_____

MARCH

Would you take 3 million dollars if it meant that the person you hate most in the world gets 9 million?

20____:_____

_____

_____

_____

_____

20____:_____

_____

_____

_____

_____

_____

20____:_____

_____

_____

_____

_____

05 MARCH

What part of you as a person still needs a lot of work?

20_____:_____
_____
_____
_____
_____
_____

20_____:_____
_____
_____
_____
_____
_____

20_____:_____
_____
_____
_____
_____
_____

MARCH

What are some words of wisdom that have stuck with you all these years?

20____:_____

_____

_____

_____

_____

_____

20____:_____

_____

_____

_____

_____

_____

20____:_____

_____

_____

_____

_____

07 MARCH

How well do you know yourself?

20____:_____

_____

_____

_____

_____

_____

20____:_____

_____

_____

_____

_____

_____

20____:_____

_____

_____

_____

_____

MARCH

What is your best (not worst) flaw?

20____:_____

_____

_____

_____

_____

_____

20____:_____

_____

_____

_____

_____

_____

20____:_____

_____

_____

_____

_____

_____

09 MARCH

How forgiving are you?

20___:_____

_____

_____

_____

_____

20___:_____

_____

_____

_____

_____

_____

20___:_____

_____

_____

_____

_____

MARCH

Tell me about a time you almost died.

20____: _____

_____

_____

_____

_____

20____: _____

_____

_____

_____

_____

_____

20____: _____

_____

_____

_____

_____

11 MARCH

Are you ashamed of anything you did in the past? If you are comfortable talking about it, what was it?

20____:_____

_____

_____

_____

_____

_____

20____:_____

_____

_____

_____

_____

_____

_____

20____:_____

_____

_____

_____

_____

MARCH

Do you prefer living in the countryside, in a town, or in a big city? Why?

20_____:_____

_____

_____

_____

_____

20_____:_____

_____

_____

_____

_____

20_____:_____

_____

_____

_____

13 MARCH

What's your fondest memory of a tree?

20____:_____

_____

_____

_____

_____

20____:_____

_____

_____

_____

_____

20____:_____

_____

_____

_____

_____

MARCH

14

What are some of the most pleasant
sensations for you?

20____:_____
_____
_____
_____
_____

20____:_____
_____
_____
_____
_____
_____

20____:_____
_____
_____
_____
_____

15 MARCH

Are you happy with the career path you chose or do you wish you had chosen a different career?

20___:_____

_____

_____

_____

_____

_____

20___:_____

_____

_____

_____

_____

_____

20___:_____

_____

_____

_____

_____

MARCH

16

What's the most unethical thing you do regularly?

20___:_____
_____
_____
_____
_____
_____

20___:_____
_____
_____
_____
_____
_____

20___:_____
_____
_____
_____
_____

17 MARCH

What is way more difficult than it sounds?

20____:_____

_____

_____

_____

_____

20____:_____

_____

_____

_____

_____

_____

20____:_____

_____

_____

_____

_____

MARCH

18

What job do you think you were born to do?

20____:_____

_____

_____

_____

_____

20____:_____

_____

_____

_____

_____

20____:_____

_____

_____

_____

_____

19 MARCH

What's the biggest financial mistake you've made?

20___:_____

_____

_____

_____

_____

_____

20___:_____

_____

_____

_____

_____

_____

20___:_____

_____

_____

_____

_____

_____

MARCH

What makes you lose faith in humanity when you think about it?

20____:_____

_____

_____

_____

_____

20____:_____

_____

_____

_____

_____

_____

20____:_____

_____

_____

_____

_____

21 MARCH

What was the most painful thing to hear?

20____: _____
_____
_____
_____
_____

20____: _____
_____
_____
_____
_____
_____

20____: _____
_____
_____
_____
_____

MARCH

What biases do you think you have?

20___: _____

_____

_____

_____

_____

_____

20___: _____

_____

_____

_____

_____

_____

20___: _____

_____

_____

_____

_____

23 MARCH

What are you battling that you don't tell anyone about?

20____:_____

_____

_____

_____

_____

_____

20____:_____

_____

_____

_____

_____

_____

20____:_____

_____

_____

_____

_____

MARCH

24

What luxury do you enjoy treating yourself to?

20____:_____

_____

_____

_____

_____

_____

20____:_____

_____

_____

_____

_____

_____

20____:_____

_____

_____

_____

_____

25 MARCH

What do you most like to do when you have alone time?

20_____:_____

_____

_____

_____

_____

_____

20_____:_____

_____

_____

_____

_____

_____

20_____:_____

_____

_____

_____

_____

MARCH

What is normal now that will be considered unethical and barbaric in 100 years?

20____: _____

_____

_____

_____

_____

20____: _____

_____

_____

_____

_____

20____: _____

_____

_____

_____

_____

27 MARCH

When you're gone when you want to be remembered for?

20___:_____

_____

_____

_____

_____

_____

20___:_____

_____

_____

_____

_____

_____

_____

20___:_____

_____

_____

_____

_____

MARCH

If there was a horrible accident and
you were unconscious and on life
support, how long would you want to
be on life support?

20____:_____

_____

_____

_____

_____

20____:_____

_____

_____

_____

_____

20____:_____

_____

_____

_____

29 MARCH

Do you believe in good luck and bad luck?
How about things that are lucky or unlucky?

20____:_____

_____

_____

_____

_____

20____:_____

_____

_____

_____

_____

_____

20____:_____

_____

_____

_____

MARCH

If you had a million dollars to give to any charity, what type of charity would you give it to?

20___:_____
_____
_____
_____
_____

20___:_____
_____
_____
_____
_____

20___:_____
_____
_____
_____

31 MARCH

What's something that a lot of people are afraid of, but you aren't?

20____:_____

_____

_____

_____

_____

20____:_____

_____

_____

_____

_____

20____:_____

_____

_____

_____

APRIL

If you could open a business what type of business would you open?

20_____:_____
_____
_____
_____
_____

20_____:_____
_____
_____
_____
_____

20_____:_____
_____
_____
_____
_____

02 APRIL

What can someone do that makes them immediately unattractive to you, no matter how attractive they are physically?

20____:_____

_____

_____

_____

_____

_____

20____:_____

_____

_____

_____

_____

_____

20____:_____

_____

_____

_____

_____

APRIL

03

What untrue thing did you believe for an incredibly long time?

20____:_____
_____
_____
_____
_____

20____:_____
_____
_____
_____
_____

20____:_____
_____
_____
_____
_____

04 APRIL

What were the three most important turning points in your life?

20_____:_____

_____

_____

_____

_____

20_____:_____

_____

_____

_____

_____

20_____:_____

_____

_____

_____

_____

APRIL

What animal are you most afraid of?

20____:_____

_____

_____

_____

_____

20____:_____

_____

_____

_____

_____

20____:_____

_____

_____

_____

06 APRIL

What scandal happened in your neighbor or town when you were growing up?

20____:_____

_____

_____

_____

_____

20____:_____

_____

_____

_____

_____

_____

20____:_____

_____

_____

_____

_____

APRIL

How well do you think you would handle prison?

20____:_____

_____

_____

_____

_____

20____:_____

_____

_____

_____

_____

20____:_____

_____

_____

_____

08 APRIL

What's the most awkward social situation you've been in?

20____:_____

_____

_____

_____

_____

_____

20____:_____

_____

_____

_____

_____

_____

20____:_____

_____

_____

_____

_____

APRIL

What is something that scares you on a daily basis?

20____:_____

_____

_____

_____

_____

_____

20____:_____

_____

_____

_____

_____

_____

20____:_____

_____

_____

_____

_____

10 APRIL

When was the last time you cried?

20____:_____
_____
_____
_____
_____
_____

20____:_____
_____
_____
_____
_____
_____

20____:_____
_____
_____
_____
_____

APRIL

11

What's the most peaceful/restful night of sleep you've had?

20_____:_____

_____

_____

_____

_____

_____

20_____:_____

_____

_____

_____

_____

_____

20_____:_____

_____

_____

_____

_____

12 APRIL

What's the most dangerous, thrill-seeking thing you would consider doing?

20____:_____

_____

_____

_____

_____

20____:_____

_____

_____

_____

_____

20____:_____

_____

_____

_____

APRIL

13

What's your biggest regret?

20____:_____

_____

_____

_____

_____

_____

20____:_____

_____

_____

_____

_____

_____

20____:_____

_____

_____

_____

_____

_____

14 APRIL

Is it better to trust people or not trust people?
And why?

20___:_____

_____

_____

_____

_____

20___:_____

_____

_____

_____

_____

_____

20___:_____

_____

_____

_____

_____

APRIL

What do you think your best and worst personality traits are?

20____:_____

_____

_____

_____

_____

_____

20____:_____

_____

_____

_____

_____

_____

20____:_____

_____

_____

_____

_____

16 APRIL

Who do you miss the most?

20___: _____

_____

_____

_____

_____

20___: _____

_____

_____

_____

_____

20___: _____

_____

_____

_____

_____

APRIL

What is the hardest life lesson you've had to learn?

20____: _____
_____
_____
_____
_____

20____: _____
_____
_____
_____
_____

20____: _____
_____
_____
_____
_____

18 APRIL

What do you take for granted?

20___:_____

_____

_____

_____

_____

_____

20___:_____

_____

_____

_____

_____

_____

20___:_____

_____

_____

_____

_____

APRIL

19

What's the most stressful situation you've been in? How did you handle it?

20____: _____

_____

_____

_____

_____

20____: _____

_____

_____

_____

_____

_____

20____: _____

_____

_____

_____

_____

20

APRIL

What's the most ambitious thing you've attempted?

20_____:_____

_____

_____

_____

_____

20_____:_____

_____

_____

_____

_____

20_____:_____

_____

_____

_____

_____

How often do you change your opinions or how you view the world?

20____:_____

_____

_____

_____

_____

20____:_____

_____

_____

_____

_____

20____:_____

_____

_____

_____

_____

22 APRIL

What's the biggest opportunity you were given?

20_____:_____
_____
_____
_____
_____
_____

20_____:_____
_____
_____
_____
_____
_____

20_____:_____
_____
_____
_____
_____

APRIL

What is something we should enjoy more because it won't be around for long?

20____:_____

_____

_____

_____

_____

20____:_____

_____

_____

_____

_____

20____:_____

_____

_____

_____

_____

24

APRIL

What's a question you wish people would ask more often?

20___:_____

_____

_____

_____

_____

_____

20___:_____

_____

_____

_____

_____

_____

20___:_____

_____

_____

_____

_____

APRIL

What is the saddest thing about your life that nobody knows?

20____:_____
_____
_____
_____
_____

20____:_____
_____
_____
_____
_____

20____:_____
_____
_____
_____

26

What are you most sentimental about?

20_____:_____
_____
_____
_____
_____
_____

20_____:_____
_____
_____
_____
_____
_____
_____

20_____:_____
_____
_____
_____
_____
_____

APRIL

Do you think people more people look down on you or up to you? Why?

20_____:_____

_____

_____

_____

_____

_____

20_____:_____

_____

_____

_____

_____

_____

20_____:_____

_____

_____

_____

_____

28 APRIL

What question do you most want an answer to?

20____:_____

_____

_____

_____

_____

_____

20____:_____

_____

_____

_____

_____

_____

20____:_____

_____

_____

_____

_____

APRIL

What are some of the telltale signs of a shallow person?

20____:_____
_____
_____
_____
_____

20____:_____
_____
_____
_____
_____

20____:_____
_____
_____
_____

30 APRIL

What do you look forward to most in the day?

20_____: _____

_____

_____

_____

_____

_____

20_____: _____

_____

_____

_____

_____

_____

20_____: _____

_____

_____

_____

_____

_____

MAY

If you could instantly learn a talent or skill, what would you want to know how to do?

20____:_____

_____

_____

_____

_____

20____:_____

_____

_____

_____

_____

20____:_____

_____

_____

_____

_____

02 MAY

When is your favorite time of day?

20____: _____

_____

_____

_____

_____

20____: _____

_____

_____

_____

_____

20____: _____

_____

_____

_____

_____

MAY

What are the best and worst things about the period of history we are living through?

20____:_____

_____

_____

_____

_____

_____

20____:_____

_____

_____

_____

_____

_____

20____:_____

_____

_____

_____

_____

_____

04 MAY

What's the most rewarding thing in your daily routine?

20____:_____

_____

_____

_____

_____

20____:_____

_____

_____

_____

_____

20____:_____

_____

_____

_____

MAY

What weird thing stresses you out more than it should?

20____:_____

_____

_____

_____

_____

20____:_____

_____

_____

_____

_____

20____:_____

_____

_____

_____

_____

06   MAY

When do you feel like you are really in your element?

20___: _____

_____

_____

_____

_____

20___: _____

_____

_____

_____

_____

_____

20___: _____

_____

_____

_____

_____

MAY

How likely are you to believe in conspiracy theories?

20____:_____

_____

_____

_____

_____

20____:_____

_____

_____

_____

_____

20____:_____

_____

_____

_____

_____

08 MAY

What are some alcohol-induced stories of your younger days?

20____: _____

_____
_____
_____
_____
_____

20____: _____

_____
_____
_____
_____
_____

20____: _____

_____
_____
_____
_____

MAY

What's the best way for someone to improve themselves?

20____:_____

_____

_____

_____

_____

_____

20____:_____

_____

_____

_____

_____

_____

20____:_____

_____

_____

_____

_____

10 MAY

What was the most productive time in your life? How about the least productive?

20____:_____

_____

_____

_____

_____

_____

20____:_____

_____

_____

_____

_____

_____

20____:_____

_____

_____

_____

_____

MAY

11

What three words best describe you?

20____:_____

_____

_____

_____

_____

20____:_____

_____

_____

_____

_____

20____:_____

_____

_____

_____

_____

12 MAY

How well do you function under a lot of pressure?

20____:_____

_____

_____

_____

_____

20____:_____

_____

_____

_____

_____

_____

20____:_____

_____

_____

_____

MAY

13

What is your weakness?

20____:_____

_____

_____

_____

_____

20____:_____

_____

_____

_____

_____

_____

20____:_____

_____

_____

_____

_____

14 MAY

What are two of the most important events in your life?

20____:_____

_____

_____

_____

_____

20____:_____

_____

_____

_____

_____

20____:_____

_____

_____

_____

_____

MAY

15

What is something you know is bad for you but you can't seem to get away from it?

20____:_____

_____

_____

_____

_____

20____:_____

_____

_____

_____

_____

20____:_____

_____

_____

_____

_____

16 MAY

What's the biggest favor you've done for someone?

20____:_____

_____

_____

_____

_____

_____

20____:_____

_____

_____

_____

_____

_____

20____:_____

_____

_____

_____

_____

MAY

How does your current morning routine compare to your ideal morning routine?

20____:_____

_____

_____

_____

_____

20____:_____

_____

_____

_____

_____

20____:_____

_____

_____

_____

_____

18 MAY

What brings you the most joy?

20____:_____

_____

_____

_____

_____

_____

20____:_____

_____

_____

_____

_____

_____

20____:_____

_____

_____

_____

_____

MAY

What are you purposefully ignoring even though you know you should probably deal with it?

20____:_____

_____

_____

_____

_____

20____:_____

_____

_____

_____

_____

20____:_____

_____

_____

_____

_____

20 MAY

What do you wish you were better at?

20____:_____
_____
_____
_____
_____
_____

20____:_____
_____
_____
_____
_____
_____

20____:_____
_____
_____
_____
_____
_____

MAY

Is there anything you did wrong for
years and years, only to discover later
that you were doing it wrong?

20____:_____

_____

_____

_____

_____

20____:_____

_____

_____

_____

_____

20____:_____

_____

_____

_____

22 MAY

What is something your parents did or used to do that really embarrassed you?

20____:_____

_____

_____

_____

_____

20____:_____

_____

_____

_____

_____

20____:_____

_____

_____

_____

What small seemingly insignificant thing did your parents, or someone else say when you were a child that has stuck with you all this time?

20___:_____

_____

_____

_____

_____

20___:_____

_____

_____

_____

_____

20___:_____

_____

_____

_____

_____

24 MAY

What is the best or worst thing you inherited from your parents?

20___:_____

_____

_____

_____

_____

_____

20___:_____

_____

_____

_____

_____

_____

20___:_____

_____

_____

_____

_____

MAY

What made you realize that your parents were just human like everyone else?

20____:_____

_____

_____

_____

_____

20____:_____

_____

_____

_____

_____

20____:_____

_____

_____

_____

_____

26

MAY

What habits do you still have from childhood?

20_____:_____

_____

_____

_____

_____

20_____:_____

_____

_____

_____

_____

20_____:_____

_____

_____

_____

_____

MAY

27

What family vacations did you take as
a child?

20____:_____
_____
_____
_____
_____
_____

20____:_____
_____
_____
_____
_____
_____

20____:_____
_____
_____
_____
_____

28 MAY

How traditionally "normal" was your family?

20_____:_____

_____

_____

_____

_____

20_____:_____

_____

_____

_____

_____

20_____:_____

_____

_____

_____

MAY

Children are often very similar to their parents. How do you want to be different than your parents? And how do you want to be similar to them?

20____:_____

_____

_____

_____

_____

_____

20____:_____

_____

_____

_____

_____

_____

20____:_____

_____

_____

_____

_____

30 MAY

What school subjects did you like and hate most when you were in school?

20____:_____

_____

_____

_____

_____

20____:_____

_____

_____

_____

_____

20____:_____

_____

_____

_____

_____

MAY

What unique game of pretend did you frequently play as a child?

20_____:_____

_____

_____

_____

_____

_____

20_____:_____

_____

_____

_____

_____

_____

20_____:_____

_____

_____

_____

_____

01

JUNE

What movie seriously scarred you as a child or as an adult?

20____:_____

_____

_____

_____

_____

20____:_____

_____

_____

_____

_____

20____:_____

_____

_____

_____

_____

JUNE

02

What irrational fears did you have as a child?

20_____:_____

_____

_____

_____

_____

20_____:_____

_____

_____

_____

_____

20_____:_____

_____

_____

_____

_____

03

JUNE

What toy played the most significant part in your childhood?

20_____:_____

_____

_____

_____

_____

20_____:_____

_____

_____

_____

_____

20_____:_____

_____

_____

_____

_____

JUNE

What are some of your earliest memories?

20____:_____

_____

_____

_____

_____

_____

20____:_____

_____

_____

_____

_____

_____

20____:_____

_____

_____

_____

_____

05 JUNE

What is something I did that you thought was exceptionally kind or thoughtful?

20____:_____

_____

_____

_____

_____

20____:_____

_____

_____

_____

_____

20____:_____

_____

_____

_____

JUNE

What new hobbies or activities would you like to try together as a couple?

20_____:_____

_____

_____

_____

_____

20_____:_____

_____

_____

_____

_____

20_____:_____

_____

_____

_____

07 JUNE

What's our greatest strength as a couple?

20____:_____

_____

_____

_____

_____

20____:_____

_____

_____

_____

_____

20____:_____

_____

_____

_____

JUNE

What could we do to make our relationship stronger?

20____:_____

_____

_____

_____

_____

20____:_____

_____

_____

_____

_____

20____:_____

_____

_____

_____

_____

09

JUNE

What is something small that we can do daily for each other to make our lives better?

20___:_____

_____

_____

_____

_____

20___:_____

_____

_____

_____

_____

20___:_____

_____

_____

_____

How much space / alone time should people in a relationship give each other?

20____:_____

_____

_____

_____

_____

_____

20____:_____

_____

_____

_____

_____

_____

20____:_____

_____

_____

_____

_____

11 JUNE

What questions should partners ask each other before getting married?

20____:_____

_____

_____

_____

_____

20____:_____

_____

_____

_____

_____

20____:_____

_____

_____

_____

_____

JUNE

What do I do that makes you the happiest?

20____:_____

_____

_____

_____

_____

20____:_____

_____

_____

_____

_____

_____

20____:_____

_____

_____

_____

_____

13

JUNE

How important is it for individuals in a relationship to maintain their own separate identity?

20____:_____

_____

_____

_____

_____

_____

20____:_____

_____

_____

_____

_____

_____

20____:_____

_____

_____

_____

_____

JUNE

14

What makes our relationship better than other relationships?

20____:_____

_____

_____

_____

_____

20____:_____

_____

_____

_____

_____

20____:_____

_____

_____

_____

_____

15 JUNE

What do you think our life will look like in 10 years?

20____: _____
_____
_____
_____
_____

20____: _____
_____
_____
_____
_____
_____

20____: _____
_____
_____
_____
_____

JUNE

What do you think would bring us closer together as a couple?

20____:_____

_____

_____

_____

_____

20____:_____

_____

_____

_____

_____

_____

20____:_____

_____

_____

_____

_____

17

JUNE

What kind of memories do you want to make together?

20____:_____

_____

_____

_____

_____

20____:_____

_____

_____

_____

_____

20____:_____

_____

_____

_____

JUNE

18

What do you think the most essential thing in a successful relationship is?

20____:_____

_____

_____

_____

_____

20____:_____

_____

_____

_____

_____

20____:_____

_____

_____

_____

_____

19

JUNE

What's your favorite way we spend time together?

20____:_____

_____

_____

_____

_____

20____:_____

_____

_____

_____

_____

20____:_____

_____

_____

_____

JUNE

What's your favorite gift I've given you?

20____:_____

_____

_____

_____

_____

20____:_____

_____

_____

_____

_____

20____:_____

_____

_____

_____

_____

21 JUNE

Where do you want to live when we retire?

20____:_____

_____

_____

_____

_____

_____

20____:_____

_____

_____

_____

_____

_____

20____:_____

_____

_____

_____

_____

_____

JUNE

In what areas do you think our
personalities complement each other?
(i.e. One is too reckless, and the other
is too cautious, and it balances out to a
happy medium.)

20____:_____

_____

_____

_____

_____

_____

20____:_____

_____

_____

_____

_____

_____

20____:_____

_____

_____

_____

_____

23

JUNE

How well do you think we communicate?

20____:_____

_____

_____

_____

_____

20____:_____

_____

_____

_____

_____

20____:_____

_____

_____

_____

_____

JUNE

What adventure would you like to go on with me?

20____:_____
_____
_____
_____
_____

20____:_____
_____
_____
_____
_____

20____:_____
_____
_____
_____

25

JUNE

What's the best relationship advice you've received?

20___:_____

_____
_____
_____
_____

20___:_____

_____
_____
_____
_____

20___:_____

_____
_____
_____
_____

JUNE

What are some things you really like about me?

20____:_____

_____

_____

_____

_____

20____:_____

_____

_____

_____

_____

_____

20____:_____

_____

_____

_____

_____

27

JUNE

What do you think the hardest thing about marriage/being in a relationship is?

20____:_____

_____

_____

_____

_____

_____

20____:_____

_____

_____

_____

_____

_____

20____:_____

_____

_____

_____

_____

JUNE

What can I do to most help us?

20_____:_____

_____

_____

_____

_____

20_____:_____

_____

_____

_____

_____

20_____:_____

_____

_____

_____

_____

29

JUNE

What do you see as your role in our relationship?

20_____:_____

_____

_____

_____

_____

20_____:_____

_____

_____

_____

_____

20_____:_____

_____

_____

_____

JUNE

What would be a deal breaker for our relationship, something you couldn't forgive?

20____:_____

_____

_____

_____

_____

20____:_____

_____

_____

_____

_____

20____:_____

_____

_____

_____

_____

01

JULY

What makes us different than other couples?

20____: _____

_____

_____

_____

_____

_____

20____: _____

_____

_____

_____

_____

_____

20____: _____

_____

_____

_____

_____

JULY

What do you think would be the best way to strengthen our relationship?

20____: _____

_____

_____

_____

_____

_____

20____: _____

_____

_____

_____

_____

_____

20____: _____

_____

_____

_____

_____

03 JULY

What are some of your relationship goals?

20____:_____

_____

_____

_____

_____

20____:_____

_____

_____

_____

_____

20____:_____

_____

_____

_____

JULY

How realistic do you think couples in movies and TV are?

20____:_____

_____

_____

_____

_____

_____

20____:_____

_____

_____

_____

_____

_____

20____:_____

_____

_____

_____

_____

05 JULY

What does a happy and healthy relationship look like to you?

20___:_____

_____

_____

_____

_____

20___:_____

_____

_____

_____

_____

20___:_____

_____

_____

_____

_____

JULY

What was the last funny video you saw?

20____:_____

_____

_____

_____

_____

20____:_____

_____

_____

_____

_____

20____:_____

_____

_____

_____

07 JULY

What do you do to get rid of stress?

20____:_____
_____
_____
_____
_____

20____:_____
_____
_____
_____
_____

20____:_____
_____
_____
_____

JULY

What is something you are obsessed with?

20____:_____

_____

_____

_____

_____

_____

20____:_____

_____

_____

_____

_____

_____

20____:_____

_____

_____

_____

_____

09

JULY

What three words best describe you?

20____:

_____

_____

_____

_____

_____

20____:

_____

_____

_____

_____

_____

20____:

_____

_____

_____

_____

_____

JULY

10

What would be your perfect weekend?

20____:_____

_____

_____

_____

_____

_____

20____:_____

_____

_____

_____

_____

_____

_____

20____:_____

_____

_____

_____

_____

_____

11

JULY

What's your favorite number?

20____:_____

_____

_____

_____

_____

20____:_____

_____

_____

_____

_____

20____:_____

_____

_____

_____

_____

JULY

12

What is something popular now that annoys you?

20____:

20____:

20____:

13 JULY

What did you do on your last vacation?

20____:_____

_____

_____

_____

_____

20____:_____

_____

_____

_____

_____

20____:_____

_____

_____

_____

_____

JULY

When was the last time you worked incredibly hard?

20____:_____

_____

_____

_____

_____

20____:_____

_____

_____

_____

_____

20____:_____

_____

_____

_____

_____

15 JULY

Are you very active, or do you prefer to just relax in your free time?

20____:_____

_____

_____

_____

_____

20____:_____

_____

_____

_____

_____

20____:_____

_____

_____

_____

_____

JULY

16

What do you do when you hang out
with your friends?

20___:_____

_____

_____

_____

_____

_____

20___:_____

_____

_____

_____

_____

_____

20___:_____

_____

_____

_____

_____

17

JULY

Who is your oldest friend? Where did you meet them?

20____:_____

_____

_____

_____

_____

20____:_____

_____

_____

_____

_____

20____:_____

_____

_____

_____

_____

JULY

What's the best / worst thing about your work/school?

20____:_____

_____

_____

_____

_____

20____:_____

_____

_____

_____

_____

20____:_____

_____

_____

_____

19 JULY

If you had intro music, what song would it be?

20____: _____

_____

_____

_____

_____

20____: _____

_____

_____

_____

_____

_____

20____: _____

_____

_____

_____

_____

JULY

What were you really into when you were a kid?

20_____:_____

_____

_____

_____

_____

20_____:_____

_____

_____

_____

_____

20_____:_____

_____

_____

_____

_____

21 JULY

If you could have any animal as a pet, what animal would you choose?

20____:_____

_____

_____

_____

_____

_____

20____:_____

_____

_____

_____

_____

_____

20____:_____

_____

_____

_____

_____

JULY

22

Have you ever saved an animal's life?
How about a person's life?

20____:_____

_____

_____

_____

_____

20____:_____

_____

_____

_____

_____

20____:_____

_____

_____

_____

23

JULY

If you opened a business, what kind of business would it be?

20____:_____

_____

_____

_____

_____

_____

20____:_____

_____

_____

_____

_____

_____

20____:_____

_____

_____

_____

_____

JULY

Who is your favorite entertainer (comedian, musician, actor, etc.)?

20____:_____

_____

_____

_____

_____

20____:_____

_____

_____

_____

_____

20____:_____

_____

_____

_____

_____

25 JULY

Are you a very organized person?

20____:_____
_____
_____
_____
_____

20____:_____
_____
_____
_____
_____

20____:_____
_____
_____
_____
_____

JULY

What is the strangest dream you have ever had?

20____:_____

_____

_____

_____

_____

20____:_____

_____

_____

_____

_____

_____

20____:_____

_____

_____

_____

27

JULY

What is a controversial opinion you have?

20____:_____
_____
_____
_____
_____
_____

20____:_____
_____
_____
_____
_____
_____

20____:_____
_____
_____
_____
_____

JULY

28

Who in your life brings you the most joy?

20____: _____

_____

_____

_____

_____

20____: _____

_____

_____

_____

_____

20____: _____

_____

_____

_____

_____

29

JULY

Who had the biggest impact on the person you have become?

20_____:_____

_____

_____

_____

_____

_____

20_____:_____

_____

_____

_____

_____

_____

20_____:_____

_____

_____

_____

_____

JULY

30

What is the most annoying habit someone can have?

20____: _____

_____

_____

_____

_____

20____: _____

_____

_____

_____

_____

20____: _____

_____

_____

_____

_____

31 JULY

Where is the most beautiful place you have been?

20____:_____

_____

_____

_____

_____

20____:_____

_____

_____

_____

_____

_____

20____:_____

_____

_____

_____

_____

AUGUST

01

Where do you spend most of your free time/day?

20___:_____

_____

_____

_____

_____

20___:_____

_____

_____

_____

_____

_____

20___:_____

_____

_____

_____

02 AUGUST

Who was your best friend in elementary school?

20____:_____

_____

_____

_____

_____

20____:_____

_____

_____

_____

_____

20____:_____

_____

_____

_____

_____

AUGUST

How often do you stay up past 3 a.m.?

20____:_____

_____

_____

_____

_____

_____

20____:_____

_____

_____

_____

_____

_____

20____:_____

_____

_____

_____

_____

_____

04 AUGUST

What's your favorite season?

20____: _____
_____
_____
_____
_____

20____: _____
_____
_____
_____
_____
_____

20____: _____
_____
_____
_____
_____

AUGUST

What animal or insect do you wish humans could eradicate?

20____: _____

_____

_____

_____

_____

20____: _____

_____

_____

_____

_____

20____: _____

_____

_____

_____

_____

06 AUGUST

Where is the most beautiful place near where you live?

20____:_____

_____

_____

_____

_____

20____:_____

_____

_____

_____

_____

20____:_____

_____

_____

_____

_____

AUGUST

What do you bring with you everywhere you go?

20____:_____

_____

_____

_____

_____

_____

20____:_____

_____

_____

_____

_____

_____

20____:_____

_____

_____

_____

_____

08 AUGUST

How much time do you spend on the internet?

20____: _____

_____

_____

_____

_____

20____: _____

_____

_____

_____

_____

_____

20____: _____

_____

_____

_____

_____

AUGUST

09

What is the most disgusting habit some people have?

20____:_____

_____

_____

_____

_____

20____:_____

_____

_____

_____

_____

20____:_____

_____

_____

_____

_____

10 AUGUST

Where and when was the most amazing sunset you have ever seen?

20_____:_____

_____

_____

_____

_____

20_____:_____

_____

_____

_____

_____

20_____:_____

_____

_____

_____

_____

AUGUST

11

Which recent news story is the most interesting?

20____: _____

_____

_____

_____

_____

20____: _____

_____

_____

_____

_____

20____: _____

_____

_____

_____

12 AUGUST

Where is the worst place you have been stuck for a long time?

20____:_____

_____

_____

_____

_____

20____:_____

_____

_____

_____

_____

20____:_____

_____

_____

_____

_____

AUGUST 13

If you had to change your name, what would your new name be?

20____:_____

_____

_____

_____

_____

20____:_____

_____

_____

_____

_____

20____:_____

_____

_____

_____

_____

14 AUGUST

What is something that really annoys you but doesn't bother most people?

20____: _____
_____
_____
_____
_____

20____: _____
_____
_____
_____
_____

20____: _____
_____
_____
_____

AUGUST

What word or saying from the past do you think should come back?

20____:_____

_____

_____

_____

_____

20____:_____

_____

_____

_____

_____

20____:_____

_____

_____

_____

16 AUGUST

How should success be measured?

20____:_____

_____

_____

_____

_____

_____

20____:_____

_____

_____

_____

_____

_____

20____:_____

_____

_____

_____

_____

AUGUST

What makes you nervous?

20____: _____

_____

_____

_____

_____

20____: _____

_____

_____

_____

_____

20____: _____

_____

_____

_____

_____

18 AUGUST

Who is the funniest person you've met?

20____: _____

_____

_____

_____

_____

20____: _____

_____

_____

_____

_____

20____: _____

_____

_____

_____

_____

AUGUST

What weird or useless talent do you have?

20____:_____

_____

_____

_____

_____

_____

20____:_____

_____

_____

_____

_____

_____

20____:_____

_____

_____

_____

_____

20 AUGUST

What are some strange beliefs that some people have?

20____:_____

_____

_____

_____

_____

20____:_____

_____

_____

_____

_____

20____:_____

_____

_____

_____

AUGUST

21

Who would be the worst person to be stuck in an elevator with?

20____:_____
_____
_____
_____
_____
_____

20____:_____
_____
_____
_____
_____
_____

20____:_____
_____
_____
_____
_____

22 AUGUST

How about the best person to be stuck in an elevator with

20____:_____

_____

_____

_____

_____

20____:_____

_____

_____

_____

_____

_____

20____:_____

_____

_____

_____

AUGUST

23

What was the best birthday wish or
gift you've ever received?

20____:_____
_____
_____
_____
_____
_____

20____:_____
_____
_____
_____
_____
_____

20____:_____
_____
_____
_____
_____
_____

24 AUGUST

What's the best sitcom past or present?

20____:_____

_____

_____

_____

_____

20____:_____

_____

_____

_____

_____

20____:_____

_____

_____

_____

_____

AUGUST

25

What's the best show currently on TV?

20____:_____
_____
_____
_____
_____

20____:_____
_____
_____
_____
_____

20____:_____
_____
_____
_____
_____

26 AUGUST

What will be the future of TV shows?

20____:_____

_____

_____

_____

_____

_____

20____:_____

_____

_____

_____

_____

_____

20____:_____

_____

_____

_____

_____

AUGUST

How often do you binge watch shows?

20_____:_____
_____
_____
_____
_____

20_____:_____
_____
_____
_____
_____

20_____:_____
_____
_____
_____

28 AUGUST

What cartoons did you watch as a child?

20____:_____
_____
_____
_____
_____
_____

20____:_____
_____
_____
_____
_____
_____

20____:_____
_____
_____
_____
_____

AUGUST

29

What's the funniest TV series you have seen?

20____:_____

_____

_____

_____

_____

20____:_____

_____

_____

_____

_____

_____

20____:_____

_____

_____

_____

_____

30 AUGUST

Which TV show do you want your life to be like?

20____:_____

_____

_____

_____

_____

20____:_____

_____

_____

_____

_____

_____

20____:_____

_____

_____

_____

_____

AUGUST

31

How have TV shows changed over the years?

20____:_____
_____
_____
_____
_____

20____:_____
_____
_____
_____
_____

20____:_____
_____
_____
_____
_____

01 SEPTEMBER

If you could bring back one TV show that was canceled, which one would you bring back?

20____: _____

_____

_____

_____

_____

_____

20____: _____

_____

_____

_____

_____

_____

20____: _____

_____

_____

_____

_____

SEPTEMBER 02

What do you think about game shows?

20____:_____

_____

_____

_____

_____

_____

20____:_____

_____

_____

_____

_____

_____

20____:_____

_____

_____

_____

_____

_____

03 SEPTEMBER

Do you prefer to watch movies in the theater or in the comfort of your own home?

20_____:_____

_____

_____

_____

_____

20_____:_____

_____

_____

_____

_____

20_____:_____

_____

_____

_____

SEPTEMBER 04

What was the last book you read?

20____: _____

_____

_____

_____

_____

20____: _____

_____

_____

_____

_____

20____: _____

_____

_____

_____

_____

05 SEPTEMBER

What was your favorite book as a child?

20___:_____

_____

_____

_____

_____

_____

20___:_____

_____

_____

_____

_____

_____

20___:_____

_____

_____

_____

_____

SEPTEMBER 06

Do you prefer physical books or ebooks?

20____:_____

_____

_____

_____

_____

_____

20____:_____

_____

_____

_____

_____

_____

20____:_____

_____

_____

_____

_____

_____

07 SEPTEMBER

What is the longest book you've read?

20____:_____

_____

_____

_____

_____

20____:_____

_____

_____

_____

_____

20____:_____

_____

_____

_____

_____

SEPTEMBER 08

What book genres do you like to read?

20____:_____

_____

_____

_____

_____

_____

20____:_____

_____

_____

_____

_____

_____

20____:_____

_____

_____

_____

_____

09 SEPTEMBER

How fast do you read?

20____:_____

_____

_____

_____

_____

20____:_____

_____

_____

_____

_____

20____:_____

_____

_____

_____

_____

SEPTEMBER 10

How often do you go to the library?

20___:_____

_____

_____

_____

_____

_____

20___:_____

_____

_____

_____

_____

_____

20___:_____

_____

_____

_____

_____

11 SEPTEMBER

What book has influenced you the most?

20____: _____

_____

_____

_____

_____

_____

20____: _____

_____

_____

_____

_____

_____

20____: _____

_____

_____

_____

_____

SEPTEMBER  12

Do you prefer fiction or nonfiction books?

20____:_____

_____

_____

_____

_____

_____

20____:_____

_____

_____

_____

_____

_____

20____:_____

_____

_____

_____

_____

13 SEPTEMBER

What book has changed one of your long-held opinions?

20____: _____

_____

_____

_____

_____

_____

20____: _____

_____

_____

_____

_____

_____

20____: _____

_____

_____

_____

_____

SEPTEMBER 14

What book has had the biggest effect on the modern world?

20____:_____

_____

_____

_____

_____

20____:_____

_____

_____

_____

_____

20____:_____

_____

_____

_____

15 SEPTEMBER

What was the worst book you had to read for school?

20____:_____

_____

_____

_____

_____

_____

20____:_____

_____

_____

_____

_____

_____

20____:_____

_____

_____

_____

SEPTEMBER 16

Do you think people read more or fewer books now than 50 years ago?

20____: _____
_____
_____
_____
_____

20____: _____
_____
_____
_____
_____

20____: _____
_____
_____
_____

17 SEPTEMBER

Now that indie publishing has become easier,
have books gotten better or worse?

20____:_____

_____

_____

_____

_____

20____:_____

_____

_____

_____

_____

20____:_____

_____

_____

_____

SEPTEMBER 18

What was the last song you listened to?

20____: _____
_____
_____
_____
_____

20____: _____
_____
_____
_____
_____

20____: _____
_____
_____
_____
_____

19 SEPTEMBER

What is your favorite movie soundtrack?

20____:_____

_____

_____

_____

_____

20____:_____

_____

_____

_____

_____

20____:_____

_____

_____

_____

_____

SEPTEMBER 20

Do you like classical music?

20____:_____

_____

_____

_____

_____

20____:_____

_____

_____

_____

_____

20____:_____

_____

_____

_____

_____

21 SEPTEMBER

What song always puts you in a good mood?

20____:_____

_____

_____

_____

_____

_____

20____:_____

_____

_____

_____

_____

_____

20____:_____

_____

_____

_____

_____

SEPTEMBER 22

What's the best way to discover new music?

20____:_____

_____

_____

_____

_____

20____:_____

_____

_____

_____

_____

20____:_____

_____

_____

_____

23 SEPTEMBER

How has technology changed the music industry?

20____:_____

_____

_____

_____

_____

20____:_____

_____

_____

_____

_____

20____:_____

_____

_____

_____

_____

SEPTEMBER

24

Are there any songs that always bring a
tear to your eye?

20____:_____

_____

_____

_____

_____

20____:_____

_____

_____

_____

_____

20____:_____

_____

_____

_____

_____

25 SEPTEMBER

What bands or types of music do you listen to when you exercise?

20____:_____

_____

_____

_____

_____

20____:_____

_____

_____

_____

_____

20____:_____

_____

_____

_____

_____

SEPTEMBER 26

Which do you prefer, popular music or relatively unknown music?

20____:_____

_____

_____

_____

_____

20____:_____

_____

_____

_____

_____

20____:_____

_____

_____

_____

_____

27 SEPTEMBER

Do you like going to concerts? Why or why not?

20____:_____

_____

_____

_____

_____

20____:_____

_____

_____

_____

_____

20____:_____

_____

_____

_____

SEPTEMBER 28

Who was the first band or musician you were really into? Do you still like them?

20____:_____

_____

_____

_____

_____

20____:_____

_____

_____

_____

_____

20____:_____

_____

_____

_____

29 SEPTEMBER

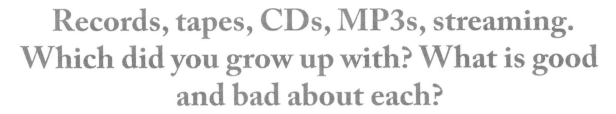

Records, tapes, CDs, MP3s, streaming.
Which did you grow up with? What is good
and bad about each?

20_____:_____

_____

_____

_____

_____

_____

20_____:_____

_____

_____

_____

_____

_____

20_____:_____

_____

_____

_____

_____

SEPTEMBER

30

What are the three best apps on your phone?

20___:_____

_____

_____

_____

_____

_____

20___:_____

_____

_____

_____

_____

_____

20___:_____

_____

_____

_____

_____

_____

01 OCTOBER

What is the most useful app on your phone?

20____:_____

_____

_____

_____

_____

_____

20____:_____

_____

_____

_____

_____

_____

20____:_____

_____

_____

_____

_____

What do app makers do that really annoys you?

20____:_____

_____
_____
_____
_____

20____:_____

_____
_____
_____
_____
_____

20____:_____

_____
_____
_____

03 OCTOBER

How many apps do you have on your phone?

20____:_____

_____

_____

_____

_____

20____:_____

_____

_____

_____

_____

20____:_____

_____

_____

_____

_____

OCTOBER

04

What's the most frustrating app you have tried?

20___:_____

_____

_____

_____

_____

20___:_____

_____

_____

_____

_____

_____

20___:_____

_____

_____

_____

_____

05 OCTOBER

What's the most addictive mobile game you have played?

20____:_____
_____
_____
_____
_____
_____

20____:_____
_____
_____
_____
_____
_____

20____:_____
_____
_____
_____
_____

Which app seemed like magic the first time you used it?

20____:_____

_____

_____

_____

_____

20____:_____

_____

_____

_____

_____

_____

20____:_____

_____

_____

_____

07 OCTOBER

What is the strangest app you have heard of or tried?

20_____:_____
_____
_____
_____
_____

20_____:_____
_____
_____
_____
_____

20_____:_____
_____
_____
_____
_____

OCTOBER

What're the best and worst things about the marketplace where you get your apps?

20____:_____

_____
_____
_____
_____

20____:_____

_____
_____
_____
_____

20____:_____

_____
_____
_____
_____

09 OCTOBER

Which app has helped society the most?
Which one has hurt society the most?

20____:_____

_____

_____

_____

_____

_____

20____:_____

_____

_____

_____

_____

_____

20____:_____

_____

_____

_____

_____

OCTOBER

An app mysteriously appears on your
phone that does something amazing.
What does it do?

20____:_____

_____

_____

_____

_____

20____:_____

_____

_____

_____

_____

20____:_____

_____

_____

_____

_____

11 OCTOBER

How often do you check your phone?

20____:_____

_____

_____

_____

_____

20____:_____

_____

_____

_____

_____

20____:_____

_____

_____

_____

OCTOBER

12

Do you text more or call more? Why?

20____:_____

_____

_____

_____

_____

20____:_____

_____

_____

_____

_____

20____:_____

_____

_____

_____

_____

13 OCTOBER

What will phones be like in 10 years?

20____:_____

_____

_____

_____

_____

20____:_____

_____

_____

_____

_____

20____:_____

_____

_____

_____

_____

OCTOBER

14

What do you wish your phone could do?

20___:_____

_____

_____

_____

_____

_____

20___:_____

_____

_____

_____

_____

_____

20___:_____

_____

_____

_____

_____

15 OCTOBER

Do you always have to have the latest phone?

20____:_____

_____

_____

_____

_____

20____:_____

_____

_____

_____

_____

20____:_____

_____

_____

_____

OCTOBER

16

What is the most annoying thing about your phone?

20____: _____

_____

_____

_____

_____

_____

20____: _____

_____

_____

_____

_____

_____

20____: _____

_____

_____

_____

_____

17 OCTOBER

How do you feel if you accidentally leave your phone at home?

20___:_____

_____

_____

_____

_____

20___:_____

_____

_____

_____

_____

20___:_____

_____

_____

_____

_____

OCTOBER 18

What kind of case do you have for your phone?

20___:_____

_____

_____

_____

_____

20___:_____

_____

_____

_____

_____

_____

20___:_____

_____

_____

_____

_____

19 OCTOBER

What was your first smartphone? How did you feel when you got it?

20____: _____

_____

_____

_____

_____

20____: _____

_____

_____

_____

_____

_____

20____: _____

_____

_____

_____

OCTOBER

20

Do you experience phantom vibration?

20____:_____

_____

_____

_____

_____

20____:_____

_____

_____

_____

_____

20____:_____

_____

_____

_____

_____

21 OCTOBER

What sports do you like to watch?

20____:_____

_____

_____

_____

_____

20____:_____

_____

_____

_____

_____

20____:_____

_____

_____

_____

_____

OCTOBER

22

Who are some of your favorite athletes?

20____:_____

_____

_____

_____

_____

_____

20____:_____

_____

_____

_____

_____

_____

20____:_____

_____

_____

_____

_____

23 OCTOBER

Which sports do you like to play 151. What is the hardest sport to excel at?

20____:_____

_____

_____

_____

_____

_____

20____:_____

_____

_____

_____

_____

_____

20____:_____

_____

_____

_____

_____

OCTOBER

24

Who are the 3 greatest athletes of all time?

20____:_____

_____

_____

_____

_____

20____:_____

_____

_____

_____

_____

_____

20____:_____

_____

_____

_____

25 OCTOBER

How much time do you spend watching sports in a week?

20____:_____

_____

_____

_____

_____

20____:_____

_____

_____

_____

_____

_____

20____:_____

_____

_____

_____

_____

OCTOBER

Do athletes deserve the high salaries they receive? Why or why not?

20____:_____

_____

_____

_____

_____

20____:_____

_____

_____

_____

_____

20____:_____

_____

_____

_____

_____

27 OCTOBER

Why do you think sports are common across almost all cultures present and past?

20____: _____

_____

_____

_____

_____

20____: _____

_____

_____

_____

_____

_____

20____: _____

_____

_____

_____

_____

OCTOBER

Is playing the video game or playing
the sport more fun? Why?

20____:_____

_____

_____

_____

_____

20____:_____

_____

_____

_____

_____

_____

20____:_____

_____

_____

_____

_____

29 OCTOBER

Which sport is the most exciting to watch?

20_____:_____

_____

_____

_____

_____

20_____:_____

_____

_____

_____

_____

_____

20_____:_____

_____

_____

_____

OCTOBER

30

What restaurant do you eat at most?

20____:_____

_____

_____

_____

_____

20____:_____

_____

_____

_____

_____

20____:_____

_____

_____

_____

31 OCTOBER

What's the worst fast food restaurant?

20____:_____

_____

_____

_____

_____

20____:_____

_____

_____

_____

_____

20____:_____

_____

_____

_____

_____

NOVEMBER

01

What is the best restaurant in your area?

20____:_____
_____
_____
_____
_____

20____:_____
_____
_____
_____
_____

20____:_____
_____
_____
_____

02 NOVEMBER

What is the fanciest restaurant you have eaten at?

20____: _____

_____

_____

_____

_____

20____: _____

_____

_____

_____

_____

20____: _____

_____

_____

_____

_____

NOVEMBER 03

What kind of interior do you like a restaurant to have?

20____:_____
_____
_____
_____
_____
_____

20____:_____
_____
_____
_____
_____
_____

20____:_____
_____
_____
_____
_____
_____

04 NOVEMBER

What is the worst restaurant you have ever eaten at?

20____: _____

_____

_____

_____

_____

20____: _____

_____

_____

_____

_____

20____: _____

_____

_____

_____

_____

NOVEMBER

05

If you opened a restaurant, what kind of food would you serve?

20____:_____

_____

_____

_____

_____

20____:_____

_____

_____

_____

_____

_____

20____:_____

_____

_____

_____

_____

06 NOVEMBER

What is the strangest themed restaurant you have heard of?

20_____:_____

_____

_____

_____

_____

_____

20_____:_____

_____

_____

_____

_____

_____

20_____:_____

_____

_____

_____

_____

NOVEMBER

07

Would you eat at a restaurant that was really dirty if the food was amazing?

20___:_____

_____

_____

_____

_____

_____

20___:_____

_____

_____

_____

_____

_____

20___:_____

_____

_____

_____

_____

08 NOVEMBER

What is the most disgusting thing you have heard happened at a restaurant?

20____: _____
_____
_____
_____
_____
_____

20____: _____
_____
_____
_____
_____
_____

20____: _____
_____
_____
_____
_____

NOVEMBER

09

What was your favorite restaurant when you were a child?

20___:_____

_____

_____

_____

_____

_____

20___:_____

_____

_____

_____

_____

_____

20___:_____

_____

_____

_____

_____

_____

10 NOVEMBER

Where would you like to travel next?

20_____:_____
_____
_____
_____
_____
_____

20_____:_____
_____
_____
_____
_____
_____

20_____:_____
_____
_____
_____
_____

NOVEMBER

11

What is the longest plane trip you have taken?

20____:_____

_____

_____

_____

_____

20____:_____

_____

_____

_____

_____

20____:_____

_____

_____

_____

_____

12 NOVEMBER

What's the best way to travel?

20____:_____

_____

_____

_____

_____

_____

20____:_____

_____

_____

_____

_____

_____

20____:_____

_____

_____

_____

_____

NOVEMBER

13

Do you prefer traveling alone or with a group?

20____:_____

_____

_____

_____

_____

20____:_____

_____

_____

_____

_____

20____:_____

_____

_____

_____

_____

14 NOVEMBER

What do you think of tour group packages?

20____:_____

_____

_____

_____

_____

20____:_____

_____

_____

_____

_____

20____:_____

_____

_____

_____

_____

NOVEMBER 15

Do you prefer to go off the beaten path
when you travel?

20____:_____

_____

_____

_____

_____

20____:_____

_____

_____

_____

_____

20____:_____

_____

_____

_____

16 NOVEMBER

What was the most overhyped place you've traveled to?

20____:_____

_____

_____

_____

_____

_____

20____:_____

_____

_____

_____

_____

_____

20____:_____

_____

_____

_____

_____

NOVEMBER

17

Have you traveled to any different countries? Which ones?

20___:_____

_____

_____

_____

_____

_____

20___:_____

_____

_____

_____

_____

_____

20___:_____

_____

_____

_____

_____

18 NOVEMBER

Where is the most awe-inspiring place you have been?

20____:_____

_____

_____

_____

_____

20____:_____

_____

_____

_____

_____

20____:_____

_____

_____

_____

_____

NOVEMBER 19

What's the best thing about traveling?
How about the worst thing?

20____:_____

_____

_____

_____

_____

_____

20____:_____

_____

_____

_____

_____

_____

20____:_____

_____

_____

_____

_____

20 NOVEMBER

What is the worst hotel you have stayed at?

20_____:_____

_____

_____

_____

_____

20_____:_____

_____

_____

_____

_____

20_____:_____

_____

_____

_____

NOVEMBER

21

How do you think traveling to a lot of different countries changes a person?

20____:_____

_____

_____

_____

_____

20____:_____

_____

_____

_____

_____

_____

20____:_____

_____

_____

_____

22 NOVEMBER

Talk about some of the interesting people you have met while traveling. 185. What do you think of staycations?

20____:_____
_____
_____
_____
_____
_____

20____:_____
_____
_____
_____
_____
_____

20____:_____
_____
_____
_____
_____

NOVEMBER

23

Where do you get your recommendations for what to do and where to stay when you travel?

20____:_____

_____

_____

_____

_____

20____:_____

_____

_____

_____

_____

20____:_____

_____

_____

_____

24 NOVEMBER

What is your favorite piece of technology that you own?

20____: _____

_____

_____

_____

_____

20____: _____

_____

_____

_____

_____

20____: _____

_____

_____

_____

_____

NOVEMBER

25

What piece of technology is really frustrating to use?

20____:_____

_____

_____

_____

_____

_____

20____:_____

_____

_____

_____

_____

_____

20____:_____

_____

_____

_____

_____

26 NOVEMBER

What was the best invention of the last 50 years?

20____:_____

_____

_____

_____

_____

20____:_____

_____

_____

_____

_____

20____:_____

_____

_____

_____

_____

NOVEMBER 27

Does technology simplify life or make it more complicated?

20____:_____

_____

_____

_____

_____

_____

20____:_____

_____

_____

_____

_____

_____

20____:_____

_____

_____

_____

_____

28 NOVEMBER

Will technology save the human race or destroy it?

20____:_____

_____

_____

_____

_____

_____

20____:_____

_____

_____

_____

_____

_____

20____:_____

_____

_____

_____

_____

_____

NOVEMBER

29

Which emerging technology are you most excited about?

20_____:_____

_____

_____

_____

_____

20_____:_____

_____

_____

_____

_____

20_____:_____

_____

_____

_____

_____

30 NOVEMBER

What sci-fi movie or book would you like the future to be like?

20____:_____

_____

_____

_____

_____

20____:_____

_____

_____

_____

_____

20____:_____

_____

_____

_____

DECEMBER

01

What do you think the next big technological advance will be?

20____:_____

_____

_____

_____

_____

20____:_____

_____

_____

_____

_____

20____:_____

_____

_____

_____

_____

02 DECEMBER

What technology from a science fiction movie would you most like to have?

20____: _____

_____

_____

_____

_____

20____: _____

_____

_____

_____

_____

_____

20____: _____

_____

_____

_____

_____

DECEMBER

03

What problems will technology solve in the next 5 years?

20____:_____

_____

_____

_____

_____

20____:_____

_____

_____

_____

_____

_____

20____:_____

_____

_____

_____

_____

04 DECEMBER

#VALUE!

20___:_____

_____

_____

_____

_____

_____

20___:_____

_____

_____

_____

_____

_____

20___:_____

_____

_____

_____

_____

DECEMBER

05

What piece of technology would look like magic or a miracle to people in medieval Europe?

20____: _____

_____

_____

_____

_____

_____

20____: _____

_____

_____

_____

_____

_____

20____: _____

_____

_____

_____

_____

06 DECEMBER

Can you think of any technology that has only made the world worse?

20____:_____

_____

_____

_____

_____

20____:_____

_____

_____

_____

_____

20____:_____

_____

_____

_____

DECEMBER

07

#VALUE!

20_____:_____

_____

_____

_____

_____

20_____:_____

_____

_____

_____

_____

20_____:_____

_____

_____

_____

_____

08 DECEMBER

What is your favorite shirt?

20____: _____

_____

_____

_____

_____

20____: _____

_____

_____

_____

_____

20____: _____

_____

_____

_____

DECEMBER

Does fashion help society in any way?

20_____:_____

_____

_____

_____

_____

_____

20_____:_____

_____

_____

_____

_____

_____

20_____:_____

_____

_____

_____

_____

10 DECEMBER

What old trend is coming back these days?

20____: _____
_____
_____
_____
_____

20____: _____
_____
_____
_____
_____

20____: _____
_____
_____
_____
_____

DECEMBER

11

What is a fashion trend you are really glad went away?

20___:_____

_____

_____

_____

_____

20___:_____

_____

_____

_____

_____

20___:_____

_____

_____

_____

_____

12 DECEMBER

What is the most comfortable piece of clothing you own?

20____: _____

_____

_____

_____

_____

20____: _____

_____

_____

_____

_____

_____

20____: _____

_____

_____

_____

_____

DECEMBER

13

What is the most embarrassing piece of clothing you own?

20____:_____

_____

_____

_____

_____

_____

20____:_____

_____

_____

_____

_____

_____

20____:_____

_____

_____

_____

_____

14 DECEMBER

How do clothes change how the opposite sex
views a person?

20_____:_____

_____

_____

_____

_____

20_____:_____

_____

_____

_____

_____

20_____:_____

_____

_____

_____

DECEMBER

15

Do you care about fashion?

20____:_____

_____

_____

_____

_____

20____:_____

_____

_____

_____

_____

20____:_____

_____

_____

_____

_____

16 DECEMBER

Who do you think has the biggest impact on fashion trends: actors and actresses, musicians, fashion designers, or consumers?

20____:_____

_____

_____

_____

_____

20____:_____

_____

_____

_____

_____

20____:_____

_____

_____

_____

DECEMBER 17

What personal goals do you have?

20___: _____
_____
_____
_____
_____
_____

20___: _____
_____
_____
_____
_____
_____

20___: _____
_____
_____
_____
_____

18 DECEMBER

What are your goals for the next two years?

20_____: _____
_____
_____
_____
_____

20_____: _____
_____
_____
_____
_____

20_____: _____
_____
_____
_____
_____

DECEMBER

19

How have your goals changed over your life?

20____:_____

_____

_____

_____

_____

20____:_____

_____

_____

_____

_____

_____

20____:_____

_____

_____

_____

_____

20 DECEMBER

How much do you plan for the future?

20____:_____

_____

_____

_____

_____

_____

20____:_____

_____

_____

_____

_____

_____

20____:_____

_____

_____

_____

_____

DECEMBER 21

How do you plan to make the world a better place?

20____:_____

_____

_____

_____

_____

20____:_____

_____

_____

_____

_____

_____

20____:_____

_____

_____

_____

_____

22 DECEMBER

What are some goals you have already achieved?

20____:_____

_____

_____

_____

_____

20____:_____

_____

_____

_____

_____

20____:_____

_____

_____

_____

_____

DECEMBER

23

What do you hope to achieve in your professional life?

20____:_____

_____

_____

_____

_____

20____:_____

_____

_____

_____

_____

20____:_____

_____

_____

_____

_____

24 DECEMBER

Have your parents influenced what goals you have?

20___:_____

_____

_____

_____

_____

_____

20___:_____

_____

_____

_____

_____

_____

20___:_____

_____

_____

_____

_____

DECEMBER

25

Do you usually achieve the goals you set?

20____:_____

_____

_____

_____

_____

_____

20____:_____

_____

_____

_____

_____

_____

20____:_____

_____

_____

_____

_____

26 DECEMBER

What is the best way to stay motivated and complete goals?

20____:_____

_____

_____

_____

_____

20____:_____

_____

_____

_____

_____

_____

20____:_____

_____

_____

_____

_____

DECEMBER

27

What are some goals you have failed to accomplish?

20____:_____

_____

_____

_____

_____

_____

20____:_____

_____

_____

_____

_____

_____

20____:_____

_____

_____

_____

_____

28 DECEMBER

What is the craziest, most outrageous thing you want to achieve?

20____: _____

_____

_____

_____

_____

20____: _____

_____

_____

_____

_____

20____: _____

_____

_____

_____

_____

DECEMBER

29

When do you want to retire?

20____:_____

_____

_____

_____

_____

20____:_____

_____

_____

_____

_____

20____:_____

_____

_____

_____

_____

30 DECEMBER

Do you prefer summer or winter activities?

20_____:_____

_____

_____

_____

_____

20_____:_____

_____

_____

_____

_____

20_____:_____

_____

_____

_____

_____

DECEMBER

31

What do you like to do in the spring?

20_____:_____
_____
_____
_____
_____

20_____:_____
_____
_____
_____
_____

20_____:_____
_____
_____
_____
_____

Printed in Great Britain
by Amazon